4.95

# THE GROWING SEASON

# THE GROWING SEASON

## CAROL LYNN PEARSON

Illustrations by Trevor Southey

*Bookcraft*
Salt Lake City, Utah

Library of Congress Catalog Card Number: 76-19712
ISBN 0-88494-301-1

11                          86 85

Lithographed in the United States of America
**PUBLISHERS PRESS**
Salt Lake City, Utah

# Acknowledgments

Acknowledgment is made as follows:

The Mother of the Bride: Copyright 1974 by Downe Publishing, Inc. Reprinted by permission of *Ladies Home Journal.*

The Good Ground: Printed by permission of *Ladies Home Journal.*

The Valentine, Prayer for an Afflicted Child, Short Roots: Previously published in the *Ensign*, April 1976.

Optical Illusion, The Cast: Previously published in the *New Era*, January 1971 and March 1976.

The Steward, Millie's Mother's New Dress, A Fascinating Study in Highs and Lows: Previously published in *Exponent II,* July 1974, October 1974, and March 1975.

# Contents

# The Growing Season

A wound in my roots
From a zealous hoe—

The quick demise
Of friendly weeds—

A strange new stretching
With the flow
Of nourishment
From last year's leaves.

Sun and rain
By turns appear:

Growing season
Must be here.

9

# Optical Illusion

Time is a stage magician
Pulling sleight-of-hand tricks
To make you think things go.

There—
Eclipsed by the quick scarf—
A lifetime of loves.

Zip—
The child is man.
Zip—
The friend in your arms
Is earth.
Zip—
The green tree is gold, is white,
Is smoking ash, is gone.

Zip—
Time's trick goes on.
All things loved—
Now you see them, now you don't.

Oh, this world has more
Of coming and of going
Than I can bear.
I guess it's eternity I want,
Where all things are
And always will be,
Where I can hold my loves
A little looser,
Where finally we realize—
Time
Is the only thing that really dies.

10

# Short Roots

The tree
At the church next door to me
Turned up its roots and died.
They had tried
To brace its leaning,
But it lowered
And lowered,
And then there it lay—
Leaves in grass
And matted roots in air,
Like a loafer on a summer day.

"Look there,"
Said the gardener,
"Short roots—all the growth went up—
Big branches—short roots."

"How come?" I asked.

"Too much water.
This tree had it too good.
It never had to hunt for drink."

Especially in thirsty times,
My memory steps outside
And looks at the tree
At the church next door to me
That turned up its roots and died.

# The Cast

I lost the starring part in Our Town
To Linda, a girl not half as good as me,
Who kept her eyes down
For the whole tryout, and even stuttered.

When the cast was posted
And the high school drama coach
Saw me reading it through my tears,
He put an arm around me and said,
"Now, look—things are not always as they
    appear.
This is not Broadway;
It's an educational institution.
We're here for two reasons—to put on a show,
And, more important, to help people grow.
Someday you'll see."

So Linda played Emily,
And she didn't even stutter.
And I was Third Woman at the Wedding,
Watching and wondering how he knew
What she could really do
If she had the chance.

Since then I have guessed that God,
Being a whole lot smarter
Than my high school drama coach,
Might be offstage sometimes
With an arm around a questioning cast:
"Now, don't try to outguess me.
Sometimes the first shall be last
And the last shall be first,
And I've got my own reasons.
I need some strong ones to star

And some strong ones to stand back.
And I'm going to put out front
Some you might not choose,
But you'll see what they can really do
When they have the chance.
Mortality is an educational institution.
We've got to put on the show,
And, too, we've got to help people grow."

As I walk through the scenes,
Watch the costumes move,
And listen to the lines
Of the powerful, the weak,
The rich, the poor,
I look at the leads with less awe than most,
And at the spear-carriers with more.

13

# Our American Family

A bell rings morning,
Calling the nation to family prayer—
Calling the many-million children to kneel
Each by his individual chair
Drawn close.

The house has seen
Two hundred years
Of births and deaths and breaths between:

The good times when the table was full
And there was singing after supper.
And the bad times when there was
Not even a chicken wing to divide.
Those were the nights the children
Lay in bed and cried.

The building times
When the new rooms to the west were added on
And there never was such a view.
Oh, the bright times when the books
And the chemistry sets came out,
And the paints—and the children drew
Their dreams and hung them on the walls.

And the dark times,
The quarreling times
When toys lay wrecked upon the floor
And the door in the hall was locked,
Dividing the house.
Or the times the kids across the street
Came with cannons and were met with bombs
And the whole neighborhood smouldered
And smoked for days.

14

After the mending of the walls
Some came back to school
To show and tell of wounds within, without,
And some didn't come back at all.

The house has held for two hundred years,
And every now and then the many-million children
Kneel each by his individual chair—
To find again the Father
And get a little good advice for the coming day—
To remember again the Mother
Whose arms are just an arm's length away—
And to recognize a circle full
Of brothers and of sisters
That always looked familiar
But they weren't quite sure from where.

The bell rings morning,
And sunrise brings the nation to its knees
For family prayer.

15

# Haiku from a
# Male Chauvinist Deer

Shameless doe leaping
The fields at full speed—making
A buck of herself.

# Eve's Meditation

Trunk and leaf
Make the tree,
Body and wing
Make the bee.

Gazing at the garden
I cannot think it odd
That you and I together
Make the image of God.

16

# At the Church Christmas Party

My little Johnny, who was three,
Climbed with lights in his eyes onto Santa's knee.
"And what would you like this year, my boy?
If I can I'll bring your favorite toy."

Johnny didn't even need time to think.
"I want a dolly," he said, "that will eat and
     drink."
Twelve parents, at least, turned to look at me,
And a big man said suspiciously,

"Next year he'll want a dress or two."
I replied, "It's the father in him coming through."
"Well, that's not what some folks would say.
A kid's character's built by the way he'll play."

My little Johnny, who was three,
Climbed with lights in his eyes from Santa's knee.
And the big man grinned as he watched his son
Ask Santa Claus for a tank and a gun.

# On Nest Building

Mud is not bad for nest building.
Mud and sticks
And a fallen feather or two will do
And require no reaching.
I could rest there, with my tiny ones,
Sound for the season, at least.

But—
If I may fly awhile—
If I may cut through a sunset going out
And a rainbow coming back,
Color upon color sealed in my eyes—
If I may have the unboundaried skies
For my study,
Clouds, cities, rivers for my rooms—
If I may search the centuries
For melody and meaning—
If I may try for the sun—

I shall come back
Bearing such beauties
Gleaned from God's and man's very best.
I shall come filled.

And then—
Oh, the nest that I can build!

# The Steward

Heber looked at his lands
And he was pleased.
He'd be leaving them tomorrow, and his hands
Hurt with anticipated idleness.
But he knew there was no other way
When a man is seventy-eight and has to make
Two rest stops with a full bucket of milk
Between the barn and the kitchen.
Condominiums—do they have gardens? he
  wondered.
His son had arranged the place for them in town
And he was ready. He sat down
On the rock that knew his body
Better than the front room chair.

Could it really be fifty-five years ago
That sitting right there
They had talked?
His father's voice had never left him:
"Heber, I'm trusting to you
The most precious thing I've got.
I worked hard for this land. You know all about
The crickets and the Indians and the drought,
And the buckets of sweat it took
To make what you see today.
I'm giving it to you as a stewardship, son.
And when your time with the land is done
And we get together again
I'm going to call you to account.
I'm going to say, 'Heber, did you make it more
Than you found it? Did you watch it
And tend it? Did you make it grow?
Is it everything it can be?'
That's what I'll want to know."

Heber looked out on the fields
That for fifty-five years had been
Green and gold in proper turn—
On the fences and the barns and the ditches
And the trees in careful rows.
Even his father hadn't been able to get peaches.
He could hardly wait to report about those.

Margaret was finishing the last closet.
Just a few things were going to the city
And the rest rose in a mountain
On the back porch, waiting for the children
To sort through and take what they chose.
She opened the lid on a shoebox of valentines.
Perhaps just one or two for memory's sake?
But whose—whose would she take?

She put the box aside and reached again.
"What in the world?" In an instant her face
Cleared and in her hands was the old familiar
        case.
The violin. She hadn't touched it for forty years,
Hadn't thought of it for twenty at least.
Well, there they finally were—the tears.
Her mother's dishes hadn't done it,
Or the little Bible she had almost buried with
        Ellen,
Or the valentines—
But there they were for the violin.

She picked up the bow.
Had it always been so thin?
Perhaps her hand had grown so used to big
        things,

21

To kettles that weighed ten pounds empty,
And to milk cans and buckets of coal.
The wood felt smooth against her chin
As she put the bow to a string.
A slow, startled sound wavered, then fell.
How did she used to tune it? Ah, well,
No sense wasting time on moving day.
If Heber should come in, he would say,
"Well, there's Margaret—fiddlin' around
With her fiddle again."
He'd always said it with a smile, though.

"I could have done it," she said out loud.
"And it wouldn't have hurt him.
It wouldn't have hurt anybody!"

He hadn't minded that she'd practiced two hours
Every afternoon—after all, she got up at five
And nobody in the world could criticize
The way she kept the house
Or the care she gave to the children.
And he was proud that she was asked
To play twice a year at the church.
And music made her so happy.
If she missed a day things were not quite
So bright around the house.
Even Heber noticed that.

And then she was invited to join the symphony in
     town.
Oh, to play with a real orchestra again!
In a hall with a real audience again!

"But, Margaret, isn't that too much to ask
Of a woman with children and a farm to tend?"

22

"Oh, Heber, I'll get up at four if I have to.
I won't let down—not a bit. I promise!"

"But I couldn't drive you in,
Not two nights a week all year round,
And more when they're performing."

"I can drive, Heber. It's only twenty miles.
I'd be fine. You would have to be
With the children, though, until Ellen
Is a little older."

"But I couldn't guarantee two nights a week—
Not with my responsibilities to the farm,
And to the Church."

"Heber, there's no way to tell you
How important this is to me. Please, Heber.
I'll get up at four if I have to."

But Heber said no.
What if something happened to the car?
And then it just wouldn't look right
For a man's wife to be out chasing
Around like that. What would it lead to next?
Once in a while he read of some woman
Who went so far with her fancy notions
That she up and left her family, children and all.
He couldn't see Margaret ever doing that,
But it's best to play it safe.
Two nights a week—that was asking a lot.

So Heber said no.
It was his responsibility to take care of her.

23

She had been given to him, in fact.
He remembered the ceremony well,
The pledges, the rings,
And he didn't take it lightly.
She had been given to him,
And it was up to him to decide these things.
So Heber said no.

She had seemed to take it all right,
Though she was quieter than usual
And more and more an afternoon would pass
Without her practicing.

He didn't really notice how it happened—
The shrinking of her borders,
The drying up of her green.
If Heber ever thought about it in later years
He marked it up to the twins.
Motherhood was hard on a woman,
And Margaret just wasn't quite the same as
        before.

She laid the violin in its case
And rubbed away the small wet drop
On her thin hand.

"I could have done it," she said aloud.
"Heber, you didn't understand.
I could have done it and not hurt anybody.
I would have gotten up at four!"

Slowly she made her way to the porch
And put the violin with the things
For the children to sort through.

"Will any of them remember?
I don't think so."

Heber gave a last look at his lands
And he was pleased.
He could face his father with a clear mind.
"Here's my stewardship," he would say,
"And I think you'll find
I did everything you asked.
I took what you gave me—and I made it more."

He got up and started toward the house,
Putting to his lips
A long, thin piece of hay.
"Better get movin'. Margaret will be
Needing me for supper right away."

# He Who Would Be Chief Among You

And he rose from supper,
Poured water in a basin,
And washed the disciples' feet.

Those hands,
Hardened by the heat of a desert sun,
Comfortable with cutting trees
And turning them to tables
In Joseph's shop—

Those hands,
That with a wave could stop
The troubled sea,
Could touch a leper clean,
Or triumphantly turn death away
From the loved daughter on Jairus' couch—

Those hands,
That could gesture the heavens open—
Poured water in a basin
And washed the disciples' feet.

The lesson lies unlearned
But to a few,
Who trust the paradox
And hear the call:

"He who would be chief among you,
Let him be the servant of all."

# The Enlightened

Her address on women's rights was marvelous.
"For centuries we were property, like a plow,
Bought and sold and used and put away.
But our women's hearts beat on, and waited, and
        now—

"At last enlightenment engulfs the world.
We do not move with man's permission, and we
Aren't disposed of at man's convenience.
We are sovereign—and our hearts beat free!"

On her way home she stopped at the clinic,
And from her darkness casually tore
And disposed of that inconvenient, waiting one,
Whose heart had been started seven weeks
        before.

# A Fascinating Study in Highs and Lows

Half a million people come there
Every year to see the view.
In fact, the pictures
On the postcards she had bought
Were taken from this very spot.

Her husband opened the door
And took her hand.
Rocks and sand
Found their way through
The straps of her little shoe,
And the wind blew
A curl out of place.
Her finger touched her face
And felt a frown.
"Oh, dear," she said.
"It looks such a long way down."

"There are railings," he said,
"And it's just a short walk.
Everyone says the view is great."
She took his arm, then faltered.
"I know," she smiled up at him.
"You go. I'll just sit here and wait."

He started to speak,
But with a girlish giggle
She kissed him on the cheek
And said, "Now don't be mad
At your little wife. I've always had
This awful fear of falling.
Oh, how can I expect you to understand—
You're so brave and strong.

I'll just sit here.
You won't be long."

He turned her around.
"No. That wouldn't be any fun."
And he followed her back to the car,
For they were one.

They sat together a moment
While thirty-three people passed by
Of the half a million that come there
Every year to see the sights.

> *"And shall we try for heaven, my love?"*
> *"Oh, dear, you know I've always been—*
> *so afraid of heights!"*

# The Ninth Month

Being a duplex,
I have been happy, my dear,
To loan you half the house,
Rent-free and furnished
As best I could.

You have been a good
Tenant, all in all,
Quiet, yet comfortably there,
Tapping friendly on the wall.

But I hear
You have outgrown the place
And are packing up to move.
Well, I will miss
The sweet proximity.
But we will keep in touch.
There are bonds, my dear,
That reach beyond a block,
Or a mile, or a hemisphere,
Born of much love and labor.

I approve the move,
And gladly turn from landlady
To neighbor.

# Prayer of the
# Young and Single

Of terrorless death I have one request,
To which a sole fear leads me:
If I may not die with the weight of years—
Take me now, before someone needs me.

# From the Mother
# of the Bride

A new family is built
Upon the ruins of the old.
The archeology is clear
And the comfort is cold.

With history as teacher
I turn accepting eyes
On the dissolving of my house—
So that yours may rise.

# Diapering at 4:00 A.M.

I saw a calf born once.
It really was amazing
How soon (all tidied up by tongue)
He wobbled off,
And the new mother
Went back to grazing.

But you, my little creature
At the top of the animal kingdom,
You would lie in the pasture for months,
And wave your fists and cry.

And so here we are,
You and I,
Tied together in all
The bathings and the dryings,
The pickings up and the puttings down,
And the turnings over,
The dressings and the undressings,
And the powderings and the feedings,
And the cleanings up of the comings out.

I know—
I know what it's all about,
This disguised blessing of unavoidable touch,
Spinning a thousand threads
That encircle us like little lariats.
And before you know it,
We're caught.

Calves come for going.
But not—not my little ones.

The Lord thought it all up,

This essential intimacy.
And he called it good.
He created the heavens and the earth,
And the seas, and the naked, needing
Infants crying to be held.
He thought it all up,
This clever stratagem.

And yet—
I'll bet he smiled
When he thought about diapering at 4:00 A.M.

# Prayer for an Afflicted Child

And now that I have fully
Informed you of his needs—
Have written out the remedy,
As doctor to pharmacist—
I have remembered.

I am an apprentice
Instructing the master.
Forgive me.
I will take the prescription
That you sign.

He was your child,
I have remembered,
Before he was mine.

# To a Child Gone

I thought I was ahead of you in line.
You would take your turn
After I took mine,
Like we did before.

I guess you don't need new shoes
For starting heaven,
Or a light left on against the dark
The way I always did.
But I'm so used to parenting.
I wanted just to be there—
To do whatever needed to be done.

But you went first.
And now, my little one,
Suddenly you are my senior.
Morning, I know, will come.
But, bring close your light—
This time it is I who fear the night.

# Spring Is Only for Beginnings

Our love
Was a blossom,
Full and faultless
On the tree.
But when the petals
Began to fall,
All
You could see
Were the sad
Leaves scattered
On the ground.

You did not
Think to watch
For autumn
When the fruit
Is found.

37

# Forgetting

Why must all memories
Stay on?

Why can't some go
In quick eclipse
Like a shooting star—
And beautifully
Be gone?

# At Sea

One wrecked at sea
May die of thirst
Or die of drink.
I always thought
I would refuse
The generous cup.

But,
Oh, my love—
I find a salted sip
Still holds some power
To satisfy.

I cannot choose today
To die.

# From the Grammarian

Putting you
In the past tense
Was, I'm afraid,
The hardest
Conjugation
I ever made.

# Acclimated

Can you become
Acclimated to pain?
Can the shiver cease,
And some condition
Almost comfortable set in?

The polar bear has been
So long a resident of frost
That the ice he walks barefoot
Is not reported to the brain.

Can you become
Acclimated to pain?

# Together

Perhaps we can be together there,
In that next place
Where bodies are so pure
They pass through planets—

Perhaps there,
Where the light that lighteth the sun
Is kept on all night every night,
And no one watches for morning
Holding the cold off with a candle—

There, perhaps,
Where pain is exchanged
For peace and a memory—

You and I can touch as we pass
And gather in the good of one another.
We can love and give
In whatever loving, giving ways
There finally are.

We still will wish
To be together then, I think.
Perhaps then we shall know how.
Perhaps, even, we shall know why
We cannot be together now.

# Good Ground

I have seen love,
Fallen on unbroken ground,
Blow with the first wind.

I have seen love,
Laid in a shallow row,
Unearthed with the lightest rain.

But pain
Is a plow
That opens earth for planting.

My heart is ready now.
Hurt-furrowed, it has depths
Designed for sowing.

Oh, love that lands here
Finds good ground for growing.

# Time for the Gulls

It's time, Father,
For the gulls, I think.

My arms shake
From flailing my field.
I sink,
Broken as the little stalks
Beneath their devouring burden.

I yield it all to you,
Who alone can touch all things.
It's time, Father,
For the gulls.

I will be still,
And listen for their wings.

42

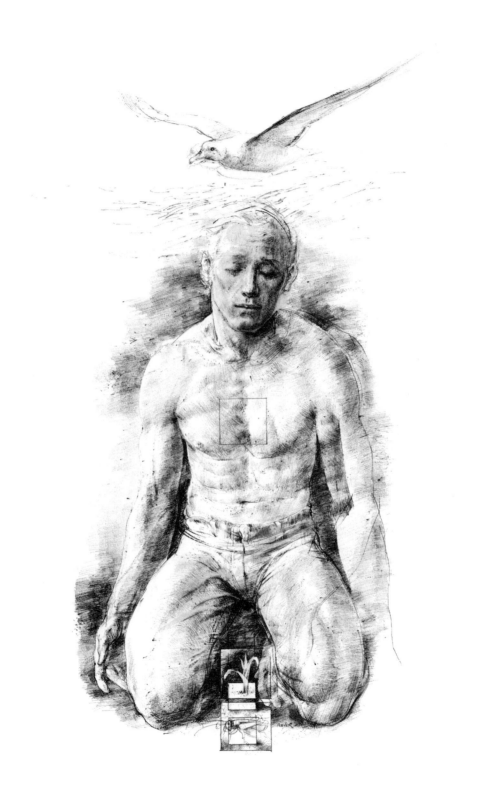

# The Valentine

I loved
The valentines we made in school.
I never cut the hearts out flat—
The two sides would never match for me.
I always folded and centered
And scissored out a half a heart
That opened into perfect symmetry.
So they never had a side that was fat
And a side that was skinny.
I loved them for that.

I felt sort of nice and tidy that way
The day we saw the shape of our being one—
As if it had opened from some good design
That made two matching halves,
Yours and mine.

But I find we don't stay put like paper.
We are not comfortable with glue.
Your edges have shifted, stretched,
And mine have too—
But not to a pattern.
If we folded our halves up today
They would not fit.
Occasionally I itch for the scissors,
I will admit.

Ah, well!
I will put away childish things—
Cut them off like braids.
We are no valentine, you and I.
We are something so alive, so moving,
So growing, I can not yet
Put a name to the shape.

**44**

I only know it goes on and on and on,
Pressing toward whatever border
There may somewhere be.

Your center and mine are one,
And between the halves there is flow.
That is much.
I will let the edges go.

# To One Who Waited

I could have
Come to you before.
But the fields in me
Wanted a little greening.
I needed
Just to work on spring
A little more.

Well,
I did.
April blossomed into May.
And every early
Bud you glimpsed—
Look:
Each a bouquet.

# Next to Godliness

There are cobwebs behind my washing machine.
I never see them except when I lean
Over to take out the ironing board
Or to put it away.
And then there they are—
An incriminating network, thin and grey.

One day
In a fit of pride, I said to myself,
"Look here, cleanliness is next to godliness,
And a mere half hour would make the backside
Of your washing machine so clean
You could eat off it."

I ran toward the closet
For the rags and soap and mop.
But I had to pass by the bookcase on the way,
And right there on top—
Oh, you know the rest.

Well,
There still are cobwebs behind my washing
        machine.
But when I lean
Over to take out the ironing board
Or to put it away,
There is a thought that consoles:

Heaven's got to be more
Than a place scrubbed clean
For a bunch of cob-webbed souls.

47

# The Honor

At two in the morning Luana May was nearly
    done.
If she used up the scraps she could get one
More that looked as good as the rest of them.
She twisted the wires of the artificial green
Around the carnation and pinched it into a stem.

The other women had helped until midnight,
But Luana May had sent them home.
After all, she was head of the women's committee
For the church and it just didn't seem right
To make them all stay up,
So she insisted on finishing the job alone.

Into the typewriter went the final card.
She flexed her fingers and began:
"This fragrant flower comes to say . . ."
She finished the last line,
Took a moment to rub the back of her neck
Where the muscles hurt,
Then attached the card to the final flower
With the final pin.

"If you want a job done right
Just get the ladies to do it,"
Brother Nelson had said with a grin.
"Like I always say—where would we be
If it weren't for you?"

Luana May
Missed most of the program the following day—
The songs of the children
And Brother Nelson's talk.

Her husband's elbow woke her just in time
To reach out and accept the corsage.
She pulled out the card:
"This fragrant flower comes to say
How we honor you on this Mother's Day!"

She looked up at the bright young man
Holding the basket in the aisle.
"Why, thank you. Thank you very much,"
She said with a smile.

49

# Millie's Mother's Red Dress

It hung there in the closet
While she was dying, Mother's red dress,
Like a gash in the row
Of dark, old clothes
She had worn away her life in.

They had called me home,
And I knew when I saw her
She wasn't going to last.

When I saw the dress, I said,
"Why, Mother—how beautiful!
I've never seen it on you."

"I've never worn it," she slowly said.
"Sit down, Millie—I'd like to undo
A lesson or two before I go, if I can."

I sat by her bed,
And she sighed a bigger breath
Than I thought she could hold.
"Now that I'll soon be gone,
I can see some things.
Oh, I taught you good—but I taught you wrong."

"What do you mean, Mother?"

"Well—I always thought
That a good woman never takes her turn,
That she's just for doing for somebody else.
Do here, do there, always keep
Everybody else's wants tended and make sure
Yours are at the bottom of the heap.

Maybe someday you'll get to them,
But of course you never do.
My life was like that—doing for your dad,
Doing for the boys, for your sisters, for you."

"You did—everything a mother could."

"Oh, Millie, Millie, it was no good—
For you—for him. Don't you see?
I did you the worst of wrongs.
I asked nothing—for me!

"Your father in the other room,
All stirred up and staring at the walls—
When the doctor told him, he took
It bad—came to my bed and all but shook
The life right out of me. 'You can't die,
Do you hear? What'll become of me?
What'll become of me?'
It'll be hard, all right, when I go.
He can't even find the frying pan, you know.

"And you children.
I was a free ride for everybody, everywhere.
I was the first one up and the last one down
Seven days out of the week.
I always took the toast that got burned,
And the very smallest piece of pie.
I look at how some of your brothers treat their
    wives now,
And it makes me sick, 'cause it was me
That taught it to them. And they learned.
They learned that a woman doesn't

Even exist except to give.
Why, every single penny that I could save
Went for your clothes, or your books,
Even when it wasn't necessary.
Can't even remember once when I took
Myself downtown to buy something beautiful—
For me.

"Except last year when I got that red dress.
I found I had twenty dollars
That wasn't especially spoke for.
I was on my way to pay it extra on the washer.
But somehow—I came home with this big box.
Your father really gave it to me then.
'Where you going to wear a thing like that to—
Some opera or something?'
And he was right, I guess.
I've never, except in the store,
Put on that dress.

"Oh, Millie—I always thought if you take
Nothing for yourself in this world,
You'd have it all in the next somehow.
I don't believe that anymore.
I think the Lord wants us to have something—
Here—and now.

"And I'm telling you, Millie, if some miracle
Could get me off this bed, you could look
For a different mother, 'cause I would be one.
Oh, I passed up my turn so long
I would hardly know how to take it.
But I'd learn, Millie.
I would learn!"

It hung there in the closet
While she was dying, Mother's red dress,
Like a gash in the row
Of dark, old clothes
She had worn away her life in.

Her last words to me were these:
"Do me the honor, Millie,
Of not following in my footsteps.
Promise me that."

I promised.
She caught her breath,
Then Mother took her turn
In death.

# To an Aged Parent

"Here, Dad—
Let's tuck in the napkin,
Just in case."

> The spoon makes its
> Hazardous trip to your mouth,
> And you glance at my face
> To see if I notice.

"All clean?
Grab hold, then—up you come."

> I dry your body from the bath
> And tell of things I saw downtown
> To turn your mind from modesty.

"Now, if you need something
Just ring the bell.
I'll leave the door a little open
And turn on the hall light.
Good night."

> You close your eyes
> And curl into privacy,
> Free from the indignities of the day.
> "Sister, don't ever grow old,"
> You used to say.
> And here you are.

> Oh, Daddy, Daddy—
> There's no way to stop it
> Or to slow it.
> Let's just let it be.

Time's strange circle
Has brought around your turn
To be comforted, and cleaned,
And nursed.
Shhhhhhh—It's all right.
Let me hold you warm
In your last days,
As you did me in my first.

# Instructions upon Admission to Mortality

Life is a labor table
From which no one rises alive.
There is peace, even pleasure,
Then pain, spaced for surprise.

Work with it, not against it.
It may help to hold the hand
Of a friend,
Or to turn up the music.
Take nothing for a quick and easy end.

You are the bearer
And you are the born.
Carefully—reverently
Approach that ultimate
Delivery.

57

# The Late Afternoon Prayer of Clara Louise

So, Heavenly Father,
You've got to do something.
You know I don't bother you
Except when I'm desperate.
And I *am*—I just can't—

    Crying out loud,
    Who's at the door?
    I've been two weeks or more
    Working up to a prayer,
    And now somebody's knocking.

    It's Beth Ellen.
    What in the world does *she* want?
    Never see her for months at a time,
    And then there she is wanting something.
    Still hasn't brought back those
    Fifteen canning jars I loaned her
    When the rain knocked her peaches off
    All at once that day.
    And she never even called up to say
    Thanks the time I hurried over
    With the ice cubes
    When she'd had all those teeth out.

    Why should I answer it?
    It's not as if she comes over
    Just to visit ever.
    It's not as if she likes me.

    There, she's turning away.
    Good.

Well, Heavenly Father,
You've just got to answer me.
It's not as if I bother you a lot,
You know I don't.
And if I could
I'd take care of it myself and just let you be.
But I don't know how.

So here I am, Heavenly Father.
Help me—
Now!

# The Proficient Prayer

I'm getting very
Proficient at praying,
I will admit.

I give the prayer,
And I answer it.

# All Us Millions

Divided by darkness,
Blended by the sun—
Through some amazing mathematics,
We come out—
One.

60

# Our Heart's in the Barnyard

The senator's wife is arrested
For drunken driving,
And the news rooms tap out applause
From coast to coast.

A celebrated marriage ends,
And the cameras crane to get
Close enough to catch the death
In living color.

A chicken takes sick
And a dozen friends come quick,
To peck past the last
Shiver in the reddening mud.

Barnyard creatures
Have such a taste for blood.

61

# Conversation with a Gentleman in Jerusalem

"I'm here to build a hotel," he said,
As we sat on a bench by the Garden Tomb.
"Right up on top of the Mount of Olives.
    Five hundred rooms."

"On top of the Mount of Olives?" I asked.
"Why, sure—best spot I ever saw.
Fact, I'm surprised that no one's beat me
    To the draw.

"We'll have picture postcards in every desk,
With a glued-on piece of an olive tree—
To prove to the folks that you practically slept
    In Gethsemane."

"Uh—there's just one thing that worries me,"
I said to the man. "Could you explain
What happens when the Mount of Olives
    Is cleft in twain?"

"Cleft in what?" He looked at me
As blank as the blue Jerusalem sky.
"It's not going to cleft. Well, I'd just like
    To see it try."

Before he left he examined the tomb,
Memorized size and shape. I guess
The only thing he didn't see was its
    Amazing emptiness.

# Vital Signs

How presumptuous we mortals are—
Pronouncing one another dead
Because the eyes are closed,
The lips are stilled,
There is no motion in the narrow bed.

A man once came
To clear our definitions.
He knew all words, all places,
All states of being,
For he had traveled below all things
And above.

"Death," he said, "is darkness, is hate."
"And life," he said, "is light, is love."

Oh, look again.
A vital sign burns bright and gives
This word:

She loved, she loves, she yet will love.
And Love pronounces that she lives.

# The Family of Light

Kindled into the family
That sparked the sun,
We came—
With suns and moons and stars
In us forever.

And the Mother,
Who nurtures new light
In the warmest of all wombs,
And the Father,
Who holds in his hands
The growing glow and blows it brighter—
Together placed us in another room.

It is dark here.
Deep within element
We dim and dim.
And to slim the ray
That might find its way out,
We hand-craft clever bushels
Of modest, fashionable fears.

But long darkness is untenable
To one whose patriarchal line shines gold,
And we yearn for the burning
To begin again.

We have had too much night.
Shall we—
Shall we together shed our bushels
And stand revealed—
Sons and daughters of light?